Royal Copley
(plus Royal Windsor and Spaulding)
Book II

Joe Devine
Leslie C. & Marjorie A. Wolfe

COLLECTOR BOOKS
A Division of Schroeder Publishing Co., Inc.

The current values in this book should be used only as a guide. They are not intended to set prices, which vary from one section of the country to another. Auction prices as well as dealer prices vary greatly and are affected by condition as well as demand. Neither the author nor the publisher assumes responsibility for any losses that might be incurred as a result of consulting this guide.

Please address all correspondence to:
Joseph M. Devine
1411 3rd Street
Council Bluffs, Iowa 51503-6805

Cover design by Beth Summers
Book layout by Mary Ann Hudson

Searching For A Publisher?

We are always looking for knowledgeable people considered to be experts within their fields. If you feel that there is a real need for a book on your collectible subject and have a large comprehensive collection, contact Collector Books.

COLLECTOR BOOKS
P.O. Box 3009
Paducah, Kentucky 42002-3009

Contents

Dedication

This book is graciously dedicated to
Marjorie A. Wolfe
In loving memory of her husband
Leslie C. Wolfe
1918 – 1987

Without their dedication and determination, the story of the Spaulding China Company would never have been told. They have earned and deserve the credit for this story.

Joseph M. Devine

Leslie C. Wolfe and Marjorie A. Wolfe, a husband and wife team, were born and reared in Illinois. For many years they studied and collected American glass and pottery. Both held graduate degrees and devoted their lives to educational and religious vocations.

For many years they were collectors of pattern glass, art glass, Greentown Glass, carnival glass, and Depression glass. Leslie was one of the early collectors of carnival glass, and became a recognized authority in the field. He was co-founder of the National Society of Carnival Glass Collectors and founder of the International Carnival Glass Association.

Both were widely known for their promotion of American glass and pottery. They were serious collectors of all the products of the Spaulding China Company of Sebring, Ohio. In addition they were collectors of Blue Ridge China, Homer Laughlin China, Abingdon Pottery, Hall China teapots, Shawnee Pottery, Red Wing Pottery, and Hull's Little Red Riding Hood.

About the Author

Joe Devine lives in Iowa. He is a retired fire captain having served over 23 years as a member of the Council Bluffs Fire Department. He is a serious collector of all Spaulding China Company products. He is an advisor to *Schroeder's Antiques Price Guide, Garage Sale and Flea Market Annual,* and is the Spaulding China Company consultant to the *Official Price Guide to Pottery and Porcelain, Eighth Edition,* by Harvey Duke.

Preface

All of the products of the Spaulding China Company have become very collectible, with the finest pieces being in greatest demand. Had records been kept of everything produced, the preparation of Books I and II would have been relatively simple. As a result it has been a real challenge because so many varied and different items were produced. Spaulding changed production frequently and this accounts for the wide variety of items on the market. There seems to be no end of surprises.

The Spaulding China Company of Sebring, Ohio, produced three major lines: Royal Copley, Royal Windsor, and items marked Spaulding. Of the three major lines it was Royal Copley that dominated everything. Although Spaulding sold their wares to all kinds of stores it was the chain stores (the 5¢ and 10¢ stores) that handled the Royal Copley. At least 85% of everything produced by the Spaulding China Company was Royal Copley. Spaulding's success can be attributed to their motto, "Gift Shop Merchandise at Chain Store Prices."

Spaulding began operation in early 1942 at Sebring, Ohio, and continued until the factory closed in 1957. Although the factory closed in 1957, there was a time of liquidation lasting for about two years. During this time outstanding orders were filled by a company nearby, China Craft.

How we wish everything produced at Spaulding had been marked. Many items were marked with either a green or gold stamp and some were marked with raised letters. However, the majority of pieces had only paper labels. From experience we know what happened to the labels. Thank goodness, many people kept the labels intact. For some of those very unusual and varied items, it was the paper label that told us it was Copley, Windsor, or Spaulding. The majority of Spaulding's items had that common "family" feature and their identity, with or without labels, was no problem. It was the "non-conforming" designs and colors that made identification very difficult. Even to this very moment the unexpected is being discovered. So, we can expect to find more undiscovered items in the months and years ahead. This makes collecting all the more interesting and exciting.

In Book I we told the story of the Spaulding China Company and went into detail concerning Royal Copley. To avoid duplication we are suggesting

Preface

you consult or purchase Book I for that information. Book I is still the basic primer for Royal Copley and the other products of Spaulding China Company. To get the full story we feel Book I is essential. Books are available in case you want or need one.

We are continuing to feature items made in as many colors as possible. This can be very helpful to collectors and dealers when buying and selling through the mail.

As we expected, the gold trimmed items have gained a new popularity all of their own. Therefore, we have added a full page of just gold trimmed pieces. Although these items were shown in Book I they didn't have the distinction of being gold trimmed.

The matter of size can be so misleading unless one has something with which to compare. For instance, a medium-sized duck or chicken might be interpreted as a small duck or chicken unless a visual example is there to show the difference. Therefore, a few items from Book I have been used for purposes of comparison.

Book II was made possible through the cooperation and help of so many collectors. We hope you will let us know when you find new items and new colors not shown in either Book I or Book II. In this was we can share the "continuing" story.

Although we have thanked many people for their help and assistance we want to thank in an additional way the following people:

(a) Joe Feinberg for the colored slides he took at Spaulding during the latter forties — and loaned to us for Book II.

(b) John Miller for his in depth insight and articles on the Spaulding operation during 1948 – 49.

(c) Elizabeth & Charles Boyce of Indiana and Virginia & Lawrence Keefe of Illinois for making the day of photographing a time of joy rather than frustration. The Boyces drove a total distance of 500 miles to help us.

(d) The following people loaned *many* items from their collections:

    (1) Ed and Shirley Lehew of West Virginia.*

    (2) Linley and Joyce Carson of Ohio.

    (3) Warren and Barb White of Iowa.

    (4) Bob and Marjorie Thorup of Kansas. **

    (5) Rachel Osborne of Ohio.

    (6) Virginia Keefe and Mary Kay Sigler from Illinois, our neighbors.

    (7) Juarine Wooldridge of Missouri.

    (8) Sharon Adams, Beatrice & Mike Smith of West Virginia.

    (9) Rose and Jim Huffman of Nebraska.

   (10) Jack and Carol Broas of Wisconsin.

*Drove from West Virginia to Ohio to meet us.
**Drove from Kansas to deliver items to our home.

Acknowledgments

There is no way to adequately thank people who have given so generously of their time and effort in our behalf. Every author is indebted to those wonderful people who are willing to share and loan items for their collection. The following people are more deserving than any words or thanks we can offer. It was their help, encouragement, and personal interest that made this book possible.

California – Dean & Shirley Horstman, Anthony & Joan Priolo, and Claudia Wilde.

Florida – Joe Feinberg, Rocky & Carol McReynolds, Mark Supnick, and Helen Wheeley.

Illinois – Larry Alexander, Ed Ashley, Evelyn Carlson, Louie Ella Davis, Gene Ellison, Mark & Sue Fraser, Doris & Top Frizzell, Bob & Ruby Gano, Doris & Burdell Hall, Dr. Lawrence Hunt, Inez Jenkins, Alice Karnes, Virginia & Lawrence Keefe, Betty Dera, Hildegard Lary, Cathy LeGrand, Dee & Merle Long, Dorothy Moody, Eileen Mullen, Jack Murnane, Ken & Sue Perkings, David & Nancy Peterson, Lloyd & Alta Sansouci, Mary Kay Sigler, Rosalind Smith, and Barbara Lannon.

Indiana – Elizabeth & Charles Boyce and Sharon & Bob Huxford.

Iowa – Bill O'Brien, Nina K. Davis, Dennis Paul Devine, Sr., Norman Devine, Laura Erickson, Glenn Hovinga, Karen Seehusen, Warren & Barb White, and Evalee Younts.

Kansas – Jeff & Shannon Lawrence and Bob & Marjorie Thorup.

Kentucky – Allen & Pat Morris, Dana Curtis, and Tom Clouser.

Maine – Brad Waterman.

Michigan – Don Brewer, Norma & Daria Killinger, and Guy Munsell.

Minnesota – Jim Butler, Rick Harling, and Robert Harling.

Missouri – Dave & Mary Boylan Family, Phyllis Lee Clark, Jo Cunningham, Joanne Grant, Dan Huck, Patti Roerig, and Juarine Wooldridge.

Nebraska – Rose & Jim Huffman, and Bob & Judy Mohnike.

New Jersey – Judy Posner and Norma Rehl.

New York – Judith Belzer, Harvey Duke, Ed Gisel, and John S. Miller.

Ohio – Andrew Anderson, Martha Brisher, Betty & Floyd Carson, Linley & Joyce Carson, Donna Cowell, Charlotte Eardley, Mrs. Claude Fee, Ray Fisher, Margaret Kadisch, Shirley & Dan King, Anna Marie Oligee, Rachel Osborne, John Parent, Hattie Robinson, Bob Sabo, Arlene Showalter, and Betty Ward.

Pennsylvania– Mary Hall and Dennis Zerby.

Tennessee – Norma & Sherman Lilly and Mrs. Burnelle Mahaffey.

Texas – Maureen Moos.

West Virginia – Sharon Adams, Edward & Shirley Lehew, and Beatrice & Mike Smith.

Wisconsin – Jack & Carol Broas.

Royal Copley — Still Going Strong

Royal Copley started off running and it hasn't stopped! It is no secret! The time was "ripe" for a new collectible, but this alone didn't bring Royal Copley to the foreground. It was the rich, blending colors that caught the eye of collectors all over the nation. Here was a reasonably priced item that had all appearances of having come from a gift shop rather than a five and ten cents store! Spaulding's motto, "Gift Shop Merchandise at Chain Store Prices," did the "trick" in revolutionizing the taste of customers for chain store ceramic ware. Color caught the eye of collectors but it was the detail and novelty of design that finalized the urge to take it home.

Collectors have increased dramatically as more people become aware of what that "pretty stuff" really is! Those who become collectors seem to become big collectors.

Prices for the most part have been reasonable and therefore existing examples at garage sales and flea markets are quickly purchased.

Due to the popularity of Royal Copley, prices have now escalated to the point where the truly fine pieces are commanding price tags of $50 – $150 per item.

As we mentioned above, the Spaulding products have gained a place in the hearts of collectors. At every flea market, garage sale, or show collectors scramble to be first in line to find new pieces for their collections.

Some of the most sought after items are the cats, dogs, birds, horses, bears, and human faces. The action items are particularly in demand. Some examples are Dog with String Bass, Dog Pulling Wagon, Bear with Concertina, Bear with Mandolin, Cat and Cello, Cat and Ball of Yarn, and Rooster and Wheelbarrow.

Other sought after items are animals associated with some object such as Kitten and Boot, Kitten and Bird House, Kitten and Moccasin, Kitten in Picnic Basket, Kitten and Book, Dog and Mail Box, Pup with Suitcase, and Kitten in Cradle.

In every category, it seems, the more delightful an item the harder it is to find. What a pity so few special items were made. Spaulding had the best designers in the business and for that reason exceptional workmanship was lavished on their products.

The Big Two: Morris and Irving

Irving Miller and Morris Feinberg were boyhood friends. After graduating from New York University which they attended at night, they went into the importing business. They imported all kinds of items such as combs, brushes, accordions, clocks — you name it! The clocks turned out to be their best item and therefore they decided to specialize in kitchen clocks.

Irving and Morris maintained an extremely close relationship during a business career that spanned almost 40 years. They had lunch together every single day of the business week unless one of them was out of town on business.

The kitchen clock operation was called the Miller Kitchen Clock Company. As Sears Roebuck was their best customer, they produced clocks for Sears under the Harmony House label. However, most of the company's production was sold under the "Miller" trademark. The clocks were signed on the face "Miller" with a small windmill as a trademark. While they started out importing the entire clock from Europe, by 1930 they were buying the works domestically from the Ingram Clock Company in Connecticut as a more dependable source.

It appears that Morris Feinberg's first trips to Sebring were in the mid-1930s to find a pottery source for ceramic clock cases under the Miller label. In a novelty business where on clock model might be a "dog" and another might "take off" and sell like ice cream on a hot day at the fair, it makes sense that they would have wanted a domestic source that could respond to elastic demand without waiting months for a shipment from Europe. This was particularly so as they were already buying the movements in this country.

Without a doubt Morris was successful in getting what he wanted. It wasn't long until clock cases were being made at a small artware factory on East Ohio Ave. Within a short time this plant was acquired in order to control a facility that could make clock cases for the clock company. It certainly was not their intention to go into the manufacture of artware pottery.

The acquisition was made prior to December 7, 1941, since all clock production for domestic consumption stopped almost overnight with the outbreak of World War II. Brass, so necessary for clock works, was no longer available. John Miller, son of Irving Miller and a key source for this material, believes the plant was owned for a year or two before the outbreak of the war.

With the outbreak of the war, Morris and Irving found themselves with a little factory and no market for clock cases without clock movements to go inside. This is the season Spaulding started in 1942.

The Big Two: Morris and Irving

Fortunately for the operation, clay was not essential to the war effort. The country was finally coming out of the depression because of the stimulated economy and people had money to spend. The stores which couldn't find clocks, pots, pans, and appliances bought pottery and the business prospered. The same merchandising skills which had made them successful in the import clock business now stood them in good stead in the artware field.

Irving Miller had been president of the clock company. Now, with a new adventure, it was Morris Feinberg's turn to head up Spaulding.

The big two who started it all (Morris Feinberg and Irving Miller) shared responsibilities. Morris, as president, was responsible for production as well as administration of the New York office. Irving, as vice president, was responsible for sales and design. Sales included house accounts, working with three full-time salesmen, and eight to ten manufacturers' representatives. Design involved the endless new items and assortments that comprised the Royal Copley line.

When Spaulding came on the scene in 1942 planters and figurines were notable for shoddy merchandise, bad design, and bad decoration. It was the contribution of Morris and Irving to recognize that it cost no more to cast a beautiful piece of artwork than a poor one. Further, the extra cost of a first class sculptor like Anthony Priolo was negligible when spread over a production run of thousands.

Irving Miller constantly visited gift shops and the gift departments of department stores for ideas. When he saw an item he liked, he would purchase the item and inquire of the sales girl how well the item sold. Often, from an item he purchased, a new item would be added to the Spaulding line. This was the case with a pair of white chicken figurines which he purchased at Marshall Fields in Chicago. From that pair, made in Italy, came the lovely planters and figurines we are collecting today.

Irving also worked with many sculptors. However, when he found Anthony Priolo, he became the primary artist/sculpture for the firm. Everyone liked and respected Tony, a gentleman and a genius.

The Truth About Royal Windsor

Once more, we are indebted to John Miller, son of Irving Miller, for his knowledge and insight into the Spaulding operation. Having worked and been salesman at Spaulding, his experiences are both revealing and valid.

The Royal Windsor line was not an arbitrary one with different items for different customers. The line was added because of need.

Chain stores accounted for about 70% of the company's total sales. Woolworth, alone, by far the biggest customer, accounted for about 25% of the company's volume. Spaulding would sell direct to any chain of 10 or more stores.

Florists and gift shops represented a natural potential for Royal Copley items. However, most florists and gift stores reluctantly passed up the Royal Copley line down the street.

Spaulding was not set up to sell direct to smaller accounts. Therefore, in order to get this business, they developed the Royal Windsor line, selling direct to jobbers and distributors who in turn sold to florists and gift shops. To make it possible for the florists and gift shops to compete, Spaulding sold a little cheaper to the jobbers and distributors than they did to the chain stores. While many Royal Windsor items were similar, such as the French Poodle items in both lines, as a rule the identical items were never sold under both labels. Producing identical items with both Royal Copley and Royal Windsor labels would definitely jeopardize a relationship with a customer. Regardless of well intentioned plans and policies some exceptions did occur.

It is interesting to note that the Dogwood Plaque Planter was not made for the florist trade. It was designed to introduce the successful Books of Remembrance formula into the chain store (Royal Copley) outlets.

A Warm Experience at Spaulding

So often, when dealing with the history of a certain company, the inner workings of the plant are not told. It is our joy to share with you many precious insights in the day by day operation of the Spaulding China Company. Fortunately, we have been able to contact Jonathan S. Miller, the son of Irving Miller, who worked at Spaulding as a young man during the summers of 1948 and 1949. He has been kind enough to share with us many interesting aspects in the Spaulding operation. We are, therefore, going to quote his interesting story word for word as he tells it!

My first hands on involvement occurred in the summers of 1948 and 1949 when I worked as a laborer in the factory. My primary recollection after almost 40 years was the heat. The temperature every afternoon in the clay shop where the molds were filled with liquid clay was 103° to 105° F. (The casters would take a masochistic satisfaction in looking at the thermometer which hung there.) This was at the end of the plant furthest from the kiln. At the large circular kiln which ran continuously and had to be tended 7 days a week, 24 hours a day — loaded and unloaded, the temperature was 130°.

After my shift I went home. I boarded with a marvelous little old lady, Mrs. Meltzer, who was related distantly to "Gears" Cannell, the clay shop foreman. She treated me more like a son than a boarder and made me cherry pies. My room, in a finished attic under an uninsulated roof, was still sizzling with the heat when I fell into bed. Unlike the factory, there was (fortunately) no thermometer so I never knew how hot it was. It wouldn't have mattered. After my day's work I was so exhausted I probably could have slept in the kiln itself.

At the factory I worked at most of the different jobs. Far and away, the toughest job was mixing clay to make slip. The liquid clay was run through pipes and hoses to men known as "casters" who would fill and later dump 50 to 100 molds with the liquid clay. Thousands of pounds of slip had to be made each day. This operation took place on the second floor above the clay shop. It was even hotter up there. It was like mixing the world's largest cake! The clay was shipped to the plant in 50 lb. sacks and mixed in a mill which made 2,000 lbs. per batch. We carried the sacks across a long room one at a time on our shoulders to the mixing mill. We opened the sacks and dumped in the clay (various kinds of clays were added according to an exact formula). The area was always filled with choking clay dust which caked on clothing, sweaty arms, and faces. It also filled lungs and caused silicosis. The men knew the danger but either could not or would not wear the masks in the incredible heat.

By the time I worked at the plant (summers in 1948 and 1949) there was no decal or gold decorating. I recollect seeing the decorating kiln still there but not in use. The entire product was "on fire" with underglaze decoration. The Books of Remembrance were the only exception I can remember. They were produced in the last years of the Spaulding operation. I don't think there was an overglaze kiln in operation. It is quite likely another factory made and decorated these items for us on a contract basis.

Decal and gold decoration was phased out with the installation of the new circular kiln in 1947 – 48. Morris and Irving were glad to phase out decal production as any pottery factory could do it. Spaulding was always at a cost disadvantage with competitors in Zanesville and other parts of Ohio. In Sebring, Spaulding workers were affiliated with the local dinnerware union and paid substantially higher wages than workers at McCoy and Shawnee, their main competitors. Spaulding was always at the top end price wise in the chain store field. Their production costs required higher wages and the quality of design/decoration made it possible.

Courtesy of Jonathan S. Miller

Photo Gallery

Row 1: (a) 8½" Large Royal Windsor Mallard Drake.

(b) 6¼" Large Royal Windsor Mallard Hen. This pair is the most common of the three pairs of ducks that comprised the Game Birds of America Series. Signed with an impressed *A. D. Priolo* on the rim of the base. Beware of unsigned copies. $175.00 – 200.00 pr.

Row 2: (a) 7½" Large Royal Windsor Green Winged Teal Hen.

(b) 8½" Large Royal Windsor Green Winged Teal Drake. Another pair of the outstanding Game Birds of America Series. Detail and color is very good. All are impressed *A. D. Priolo* on the rim of the base. $250.00 – 275.00 pr.

Row 3: (a) 6¾" Large Royal Windsor Gadwell Hen.

(b) 8½" Large Royal Windsor Gadwell Drake. Another pair of the outstanding Game Birds of America Series. Detail and color is very good. All are impressed *A. D. Priolo* on the rim of the base. $250.00 – 275.00 pr.

All the items on this page represent some of the finest examples of work done at Spaulding China.

Row 1: (a) and (d) Royal Windsor "Baby" Mallards. $16.00 – 18.00 each.

(b) and (c) Royal Windsor Small Mallards. The baby measures from 5¼" to 5¾", and 5¾" to 6" for the small pair. Paper label only. $16.00 – 18.00 each.

Row 2: (a) and (b) Royal Windsor Medium-sized Mallards. Both possess green Royal Windsor labels. Very hard to find. The erect head is 7½" and the bending head 7". This pair is the hardest to find. $70.00 – 75.00 each.

Row 3: (a) and (b) Royal Windsor Large Mallards. Paper label only. Hen (a), erect head, is 9¼"; hen (b), bending head, is 8¾". $40.00 – 45.00 each.

All of the mallard figurines shown are referred to as a "pair" but they are actually designed as male or drake mallards.

Row 1: (a), (b), (c), and (d) Pairs of Small Royal Windsor
Chickens. The rooster is 7⅛" and the hen a little
over 6½". The only difference between these
pairs is that of coloration. Items (a) and (b) are
colored more like Royal Copley chickens with
teal colored bases, while (c) and (d) are darker
brown with light green bases and are the ones
commonly found. (a) and (b) $50.00 – 55.00
each; (c) and (d) 35.00 – 40.00 each.

Row 2: (a) and (b) Royal Windsor Medium-sized Hen
and Rooster. Paper label only. The rooster is 8¼"
and the hen is 7¾". These are what collectors
refer to as the brown-breasted pair. The medium-
sized chickens are harder to find. $90.00 –
100.00 each.

Row 3: (a) and (b) Royal Windsor Medium-sized Hen
and Rooster. Same pair as shown above in row
2, but with teal colored breasts. This pair is harder
to find. Paper label only. $125.00 – 150.00 each.

19

Row 1: (a) and (b) Royal Windsor Large Hen and Rooster. The rooster is 10½" and the hen is 10". Paper label only. Shown here in the color combination that collectors refer to as the brown-breasted pair. $175.00 – 200.00 each.

Row 2: (a) and (b) Royal Windsor Large Hen and Rooster. Same measurements as the pair shown above in row 1. The only difference is that of color. These are referred to as the teal-breasted pair. This pair is harder to find. Paper label only. $225.00 – 250.00 each.

Row 3: (a) and (c) 10½" Royal Windsor Large Roosters shown in rows 1 and 2 above. They are shown here for size comparison to item (b). NPA.

(b) 11½" Royal Windsor Rooster. Only a very few have been found. No matching hen has been reported to date. NPA.

These rooster and hen figurines shown here represent the finest and most lovely chickens made by Spaulding.

Row 1: (a) 7¾" Royal Copley Black and White High Tail Common Rooster Planter. Glazed bottom with Royal Copley within raised letters. No runners. $100 – 125.00. Very hard to find.

(b) and (c) Royal Copley Large Black and White Hen and Rooster, white base. Shown below in row 3, but not with the beautiful gold trim. Not many have been found. Priced below in Row 3 b & c without gold trim.

Row 2: (a) 8" Royal Copley Large Black and White Rooster. Paper label only. Green base. $100.00 – 110.00.

(b) and (c) Royal Copley Small Black and White Hen and Rooster. Green base. Only a few have been found. Paper label only. Hen is 5½" and the rooster 6". $175.00 – 200.00 each.

Row 3: (a) 7¼" Royal Copley Large Black and White Hen. Green base. Mate to the rooster above in row 2 (a). Paper label only. $100.00 – 110.00.

(b) and (c) Royal Copley Large Black and White Hen and Rooster. White base. Rooster is 8" and the hen 7¼". Paper label only. All black and white chickens are rather hard to find. The white base chickens are harder to find than the green base. $110.00 – 125.00 each.

Row 1: (a) and (b) Spaulding's Large Pheasants. The pheasant figurines shown here may sometimes be found with a number stamped on the bottom. The number indicates the stock number and the number of books of S&H green stamps needed to redeem these items when they were included in their gift catalog during the fifties. $40.00 – 45.00 pr.

Row 2: (a) and (b) Spaulding's Large Pheasants. This pair is brightly decorated with vibrant colors. Notice they have no ring around their neck. Harder to find. $45.00 – 50.00 pr.

Row 3: (a) and (b) Spaulding Large Pheasants. The only differences between these and the pair shown above in row 2 are the white ring around their necks and less color. All of these pheasant figurines shown measure 6¾" x 12" and 10½" x 9" respectively. $40.00 – 45.00 pr.

25

Row 1: (a), (b), and (c) 3⅝" Royal Copley Baby Larks. Paper label only. The small birds are harder to find. $30.00 – 32.00.

(d) and (e) 3½" Royal Copley Small Kinglets. Paper label only. $26.00 – 28.00.

Row 2: (a), (b), (c), (d), and (e), 3½" Royal Copley Little Wrens. Paper label only. As you can see they come in a variety of colors. $30.00 – 32.00.

Row 3: (a), (b), (c), and (d) 4½" Nuthatches. A little hard to find. Paper label only. Full bodied. Found in various colors. Notice the hand-painted mask on item (b). Be aware of a smaller, similar bird figurine that has a full painted beak. It is not Copley. $16.00 – 18.00.

27

Row 1: (a), (b), (c), and (d) 4" small Spaulding Pheasants. Found in a variety of colors, some tails
have brush marks. Paper label only. $20.00 –
25.00.

Row 2: (a) and (b) 4¾" Spaulding Grouse. Paper label
only. Notice the ring around the neck on item
(b). Hard to find. $30.00 – 35.00.

Row 3: (a) and (b) 5½" Spaulding Pheasants. Paper label
only. Hard to find, only difference is that of
color. $40.00 – 45.00.

All the items shown in Row 1 are white with gold trim and are harder to find than those colors in which they were commonly decorated.

Row 1: (a) 8" Royal Copley Seagull. Shown in Book 1 in regularly found colors. $50.00 – 55.00.

(b) 5½" Spaulding Pheasant. Two examples of regular color on page 29. $50.00 – 55.00.

(c) 7" Spaulding Cockatoo. Shown on page 37 in three color variations. $35.00 – 40.00.

Row 2: (a) and (b) 5" Doves. Paper label only. Full bodied. Found in various colors. Quality of color is a bit inferior. $12.00 – 15.00.

(c) and (d) 5" Buntings. Paper label only. Hard to find. Notice the difference in the shape of the tails. This is the key in matching a pair. Named in honor of Virginia and Lawrence Keefe of Villa Grove, Illinois, who provided help and assistance all along the way to Marjorie and Leslie when they were preparing the books. $30.00 – 35.00 each.

Row 3: (a) 5½" Royal Copley Blue Sparrow. A very lovely addition to a bird collection. Very hard to find. Paper label only. $60.00 – 65.00.

(b) 5½" Royal Copley Canary. Very hard to find. Paper label only. The only difference between (a) and (b) is the coloration. $55.00 – 60.00.

(c) 5" Royal Copley Long's Finch No. 2. Not many have been reported. It may have been redesigned into item (d) and (e). Paper label only. Named in honor of Merle and Dee Long of Illinois. NPA.

(d) and (e) 5" Royal Copley Finches. This design of the finch is the one most commonly found, although not that easily. Paper label only. $35.00 – 40.00

31

Row 1: (a), (b), and (c) 8" Spaulding Jays. A very elusive-bird much sought after by Copley collectors. Found with varying degrees of hand decorating. Paper label only. (a) $75.00 – 80.00; (b) $80.00 – 90.00; (c) $100.00 – 125.00.

Row 2: (a), (b), and (c) 8" Spaulding Jays. Three different colors than shown above in row 1. Items (a) and (b) have no hand decorating. Notice how the hand decorating adds to the beauty of item (c). Occasionally found with a Royal Copley label. (a) $75.00 – 80.00; (b) $80.00 – 90.00; (c) $100.00 – 125.00.

Row 3: (a), (b), (c), and (d) 7¾" Flycatchers. Paper label only. Very fine detail. It may be found with added hand decorating as shown in item (c). They add a lot of color to any bird collection. Hard to find. $40.00 – 45.00.

Row 1: (a) 6" Spaulding Parrot. Only two have been reported to date. *Spaulding Pat. Pending* is impressed on the bottom. A very rare and colorful bird. NPA. Courtesy of Geneva Ives of Iowa.

(b) and (c) 5¾" Pouter Pigeons. Paper label only. Two runners. Found in shades of brown and gray. Named in honor of Lillian Szafranski of Ohio. $20.00 – 25.00 each.

Row 2: (a), (b), and (c) 8" Spaulding Hunt's Swallow Variants. Paper label only. Very hard to find. Items (a) and (c) are the males and item (b) the female. Identification of these birds is very difficult as they show characteristics of more than one bird. They tend to drive any ornithologist "up the wall." They were designed to sell and not be ornithologically correct. They are positively outstanding in color and design. We are naming these birds in honor of Dr. Lawrence Hunt of Eastern Illinois University who has been so gracious in helping us. (a) 75.00 – 85.00; (b) and (c) $90.00 – 100.00.

Row 3: (a), (b), and (c) 8" Spaulding Hunt's Swallow Variants. The same birds as shown in row 2 above, but in different colors. Paper label only. Occasionally found with a Royal Copley label. The hand decorated ones are harder to find and more valuable. (a) & (b) $75.00 – 85.00; (c) $90.00 – 100.00.

Row 1: (a), (b), and (c) 7" Spaulding Cockatoos. Found primarily decorated in the three color combinations shown here. Notice that all three have different styles of hand-painted eyes and beaks. The overall quality is a bit inferior when compared to the other Spaulding birds. Paper label only. $25.00 – 30.00.

Row 2: (a), (b), and (c) 7⅜" Spaulding Double Parakeets. Item (a) is marked on the bottom with a Spaulding seal and *Pat. Pending Spaulding* in intaglio. Breast is light blue. A touch of hand decorating. Item (b) is not marked. This color variation is very hard to find. No hand decorating. Breast is light yellow. Item (c) is marked only with a Spaulding seal. A touch of hand decorating. Not difficult to find. Breast is yellow. (a) and (c) $40.00 – 45.00; (b) $80.00 – 90.00

Row 3: (a), (b), and (c) 8½" Royal Copley Cockatiel Planters. Paper label only. The cockatiel rests on a kidney-shaped planter. Item (a) has green planter and items (b) and (c) (below) have black planters. Hard to find. $50.00 – 60.00.

Prices given reflect banks that have no damage to the coin slot or bottom holes from having been enlarged to retrieve money.

Row 1: (a), (b), (c), and (d) 5½" Royal Copley Farmer Pig Bank. Paper label only. Found primarily in these color combinations. Flat unglazed bottom with two holes. Hard to find. $70.00 – 80.00.

Row 2: (a), (b), (c), and (d) Royal Copley Large Pig Banks. Size varies from 7½" to 8". Items (a) and (b) show different fraternity or sorority emblems. Item (c) is a version of Midland Buckeye. Item (d) is a personalized bank done for someone named Marge. $75.00 – 85.00.

Row 3: (a), (b), (c), and (d) Royal Copley Large Pig Banks. Size varies from 7½" to 8". Items (a), (b), and (c) are color variations of previously shown banks. Item (d) shows a bank done "For Baby." $75.00 – 85.00.

one white tee perfect
one green tee
small hole
in bottom

39

Row 1: (a) Royal Copley Small Pig Bank. Paper label only. Hard to find. Flat, unglazed bottom. Two other colors are shown in Book I on page 85. $50.00 – 55.00.

(b) and (c) 6¼" Royal Copley Bow Tie Pig Banks. Paper label only. The brown color is harder to find than the rose and blue shown in Book I on page 85. Notice that the eyes on item (b) are closed and the eyes on item (c) are open. $50.00 – 55.00.

(d) 6½" Royal Copley Pig Lamp. Flat, unglazed bottom. Made for a lamp at the factory. The middle-sized pig bank was retooled for use as a lamp. A pink and white striped version is shown below, Row 3 (d). Very hard to find. $90.00 – 100.00.

Row 2: (a), (b), (c), and (d) 7½" Royal Copley Large Pig Banks. All of the pig banks in row 2 were made for certain stores, shops, and businesses. Sometimes they can be found with Royal Windsor labels. These banks were made later and even through the time of liquidation. Two runners on the bottom. Other banks with other sayings can be found. The later banks do not have a green stamp on the bottom. $75.00 – 85.00.

Row 3: (a) 7½" Royal Copley Large Pig Bank. Green stamp on the bottom. Hard to find. Listed as No. 138 on one of the color charts of the company. Two runners on the bottom. A similar bank with white shirt and blue stripes is found in Book I. $75.00 – 85.00.

(b) and (c) 7½" Royal Copley Large Pig Banks. These two banks were also made for various stores, shops, and businesses. Made later like the banks in row 2 above. Somewhat hard to find. They are Copley banks but may be found with Royal Windsor labels. $75.00 – 85.00.

(d) 6½" Royal Copley Pig Lamp. Flat, unglazed bottom. Same as Row 1 (d), except for coloration. $90.00 – 100.00.

41

Page 42: (a) and (c) 8¼" Birds on Tree Trunk Lamp Bases. None with labels have turned up but we believe them to be Royal Copley or Spaulding. Hard to find. These lamps are questionable. NPA.

(b) 11" Deer and Fawn on Tree Trunk Lamp. A lamp base. Purchased originally at a Gamble store. Notice the little flower pots that fit down into the lamp base. The pots whether original or not seem ideal for such an item. This is also a questionable item. An example can be found with the deer and fawn on one end with only one little flower pot, also questionable. NPA.

Page 43: (a) and (b) 8" Royal Copley Birds in the Bower Lamp. Paper label only. Two lamps have been found with labels. Named in honor of Martha Brisker of Ohio. Hard to find. Only difference is color. $50.00 – 60.00.

(c) 9½" Royal Copley Rooster Lamp. Less than five have been reported and all have Royal Copley labels. NPA.

Page 44: (a) 10½" Spaulding Flower on Tree Trunk Lamp. Hard to find. Notice the Spaulding label on this lamp and the one on the next page. Listed in honor of Nina K. Davis of Iowa. $65.00 – 75.00.

(b) 8½" Spaulding Thorup's Rose Lamp. Lamps are hard to find. Named in honor of Robert and Marjorie Thorup of Kansas. $50.00 – 60.00.

Page 45

Row 1: (a), (b), (c), (d), and (e) 8½" Spaulding Flower on Tree Trunk Lamp Bases. Variations include the number of flowers and of course colors. Also some have flat tops while others (a) and (b) have more rounded tops. Paper label only. Hard to find. $50.00 – 60.00.

Row 2: (a) 10½" Spaulding Flower on Tree Trunk Lamp Base. Paper label only. Hard to find. $65.00 – 75.00.

(b) and (c) 10½" Spaulding Thorup's Rose Lamp Base. Paper label only. Hard to find. $65.00 – 75.00.

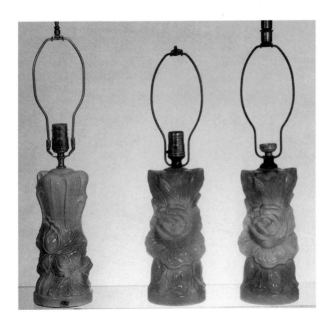

45

Row 1: (a), (b), and (c) are 8" Spaulding Decal Lamps. Notice the stylized goose or swan necks on item (b). Item (c) is shown on page 63 with different flower decals. Found with a Spaulding label. Hard to find. $45.00 – 50.00.

Row 2: (a), (b), and (c) are 10" Spaulding Decal Lamps. Item (a) and (b) are the same except for different flower decals. Paper label only. $50.00 – 60.00.

47

Page 48: 6¾" Royal Copley Hen Wall Pocket Planter. The bracket and socket has been attached through the hole in the back of planter. NPA

Page 49
Row 1: (a), (b), and (c) 10" Cocker Spaniel Lamp Base. It's difficult to tell the difference between item (b) and (c). Item (b) is a very dark green and item (c) is black. They are all very hard to find, a true lamp base. $100.00 – 125.00.

Row 2: Royal Copley Lamps that were probably home-made.

(a) 8" Horse with Mane Vase. The bottom has been drilled for a socket placed inside the planter. Notice the pull chain under the horses muzzle. NPA

(b) 8" Black Leaf and Stem Vase. Notice the four-legged base and "cap" at the top. NPA.

49

Row 1: (a) and (b) are a matching pair of 7¾" Oriental boy and girl with basket on ground planters. Item (a) is commonly referred to as the lantern boy and item (b) as the pregnant lady. Signed with raised letters on the bottom. This is a different color combination not commonly seen. Other colors are shown in Book I. $20.00 –25.00 each.

Row 2: (a) and (b) 7½" Oriental Boy and Girl Figurine Lamps. A red and blue pair can be seen in Book I. Notice the Royal Copley labels and beautiful original shades. Not easily found. $75.00 – 85.00 each.

51

Row 1: (a) 6¾" Royal Windsor Ribbed Star Planter & Candle Holder. Here we find another example of retooling in which the star and angel planter was redesigned to make this interesting piece. Paper label only. Hard to find. Can be used as a candle holder, planter, or vase. $20.00 – 25.00.

(b) 4¾" Royal Windsor Ribbed Star Planter & Candle Holder. Paper label only. Hard to find. $20.00 – 25.00.

(c) 5" Royal Windsor Valentine Plaque Planter. Gold stamp on bottom. Hard to find. Normally a plaque planter isn't too exciting but if it has a Valentine, Cupid, and arrows, it is a prized item. $30.00 – 35.00.

Row 2: (a) and (c) are 6¼" Royal Copley Barber Pole Razor Blade Receptacle. Paper label only. Outlined in gold. Several copies are showing up but they are easy to spot. The copies do not have the beading at the top; the word "blades" is in black; and detail is sorely lacking. Size seems to vary greatly with the copies. Both items (a) and (c) have original paper label. (a) $70.00 – 75.00; (c) $55.00 – 60.00.

(b) 8" Royal Copley Plaque Planter or Pocket. This is the first example of decal on an 8" plaque planter. Very unusual. Paper label only. $65.00 – 75.00.

Row 3: (a) and (b) are 8" Royal Copley Plaque Planters or Pockets. Paper label only. Item (a) reads *Constable, The Cornfield Amsterdam, Holland*, and item (b) reads *Constable Valley Farm Amsterdam, Holland*. Other plaque planters are shown in Book I. Thus far we have seen only four of these planters with Dutch scenes. Notice that this item can be used either as a wall pocket or as a resting planter. These items were designed by Anthony Priolo. $60.00 – 70.00.

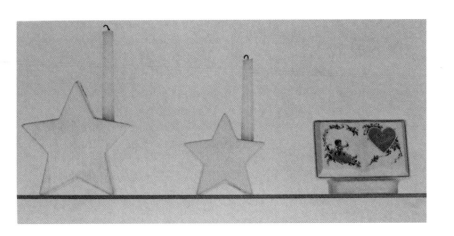

All items shown on the next page have been shown previously but without the gold trim. They are becoming very popular and highly sought after by collectors. The prices of the items listed are for regular items and not the gold trimmed ones. One can expect to pay from 25 to 50 percent more for any gold trimmed item. The gold trimming on these items was not done at the factory.

Row 1:   (a) 8" Royal Copley Floral Beauty Pitcher. Shown in Book I. $45.00 – 50.00.

(b) 7" Royal Copley Large Hat Planter. Shown in Book I. $40.00 – 45.00.

(c) 8¼" Royal Copley Stylized Leaf Vase. Shown in Book I. $12.00 – 15.00.

Row 2:   (a) and (b) 8" Royal Copley Pirate Head Wall Pocket or Planter. Shown in Book I. $45.00 – 50.00.

(c) 8" Royal Windsor Island Lady Planter. Shown on page 111. $100.00 – 125.00.

Row 3:   (a) and (b) are Royal Copley Girl and Boy Leaning on Barrel Planters. Shown in Book I. $20.00 – 25.00.

(c) 7" Royal Copley Girl and Wheelbarrow Planter. Shown in Book I. $25.00 – 30.00.

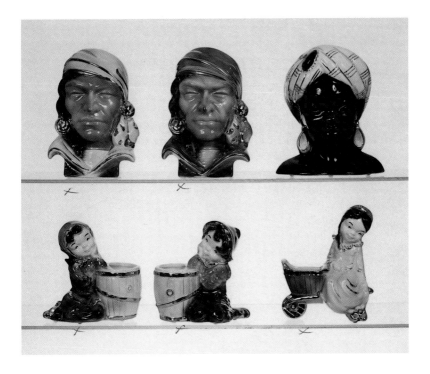

Row 1: (a) and (b) 7½" Royal Copley Swallow on Heavy Double Stump. Paper Label only. Notice how the tails differ. Item (a) is more rounded while item (b) is v-shaped. This is the key to finding a pair. 40.00 – 45.00 each.

Row 2: (a) and (b) 7½" Royal Copley Swallow on Heavy Double Stump. Same pair as above but with heavy gold trim and opalescent glaze. Very hard to find with gold trim and this glaze. They were done outside the factory. Priced without gold trim and opalescent glaze. $40.00 – 45.00.

All items shown is row 3 have been previously shown but without gold trim. Prices listed are for regular items and not with gold trim.

Row 3: (a) 8" Royal Copley Bird House with Bird Planter. Shown in Book I. $100.00 – 110.00.

(b) 8¼" Royal Copley Kitten with Ball of Yarn planter. $35.00 – 40.00.

(c) 8" Royal Copley Black & White Teddy Bear Bank. $150.00 – 175.00.

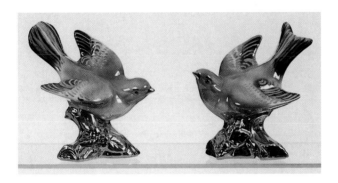

Row 1: 5¼" Royal Copley Comma Vase. This vase repre-
sents an example that was used for a new color
or glaze. The bottom of the planter is also
shown and as you can see, handwritten in black
ink, *Ex. 396 yello*. This is the only piece of Copley
that has surfaced to date with this color so it
obviously was never put into production. NPA.

Row 2: 7½" Royal Copley Chinese Girl with Big Hat Wall
Pocket. Shown for comparison with Row 3.
Shown in Book I. NPA.

Row 3: 7½" Royal Copley Chinese Girl without Big Hat
experimental piece. More than likely an attempt
was made to design a type of lamp or night lite
by cutting off the hat and the back of the
planter. Item (c) shows the bottom which has
been drilled and item (a) is a back view showing
a hole drilled for a cord. NPA.

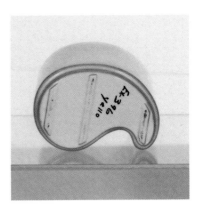

59

Row 1: (a) and (c) 6" Royal Copley Decal Vases. Unusual shape. No runners. Notice the characteristic Copley green. Item (a) reads *Happy Anniversary* and item (c) reads *Thinking of You*. Very hard to find. Courtesy of Juarine Wooldridge of Missouri. $35.00 – 40.00.

(b) 8" Royal Copley Cylindrical Decal Vase. Hard to find. More examples are shown on page 103. $40.00 – 45.00.

Row 2: (a) and (c) 6¼" Royal Copley Mary Kay Vases. Gold stamp on the bottom. Harder to find. Outlined in gold. A similar vase with decal on a cream background is found in Book I page 25. Named in honor of Mary Kay Sigler of Illinois. $12.00 – 14.00.

(b) 7" Royal Copley Virginia Vase. Flat unglazed bottom. Hard to find. Gold trimmed. A similar vase with decal is found on page 67. Named in honor of Virginia Keefe of Illinois. $12.00 – 15.00.

Row 3: (a) 4½" Small Oval Bamboo Vase or Planter. Paper label only. Easy to find. $10.00 – 12.00.

(b) 8" Cylindrical Bamboo Vase. Paper label only. This size is hard to find. $18.00 – 20.00.

(c) 4" x 7½" Oval Bamboo Planter. Paper label only. Not as easy to find as item (a). $12.00 – 15.00.

(d) 5¾" Royal Copley Bamboo Oval Planter. Paper label only. Three runners. Harder to find. $12.00 – 15.00.

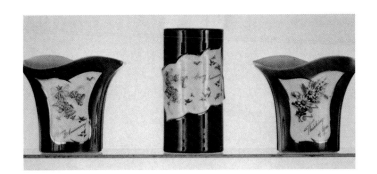

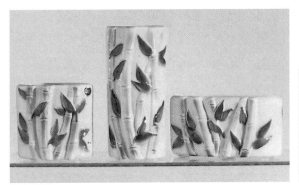

Row 1: (a) 8¼" Large Spaulding Cornucopia. Gold stamp on bottom. Used here for the purpose of comparing the two sizes of cornucopia. Not easily found. Shown in Book I. $25.00 – 30.00.

(b) 8" Spaulding Child's Lamp. No mark as most Spaulding lamps had only labels. Lovely. Hard to find. $45.00 – 50.00.

(c) and (d) 6⅜" Small Spaulding Cornucopia. Gold stamp on bottom. Hard to find. Without comparison in size, collectors might conclude there is only one size. $20.00 – 25.00.

Row 2: (a) and (b) 7" Royal Copley King Decal Vases. Flat unglazed bottom. A similar vase in rose is found in Book I. Paper label only. Hard to find. Named in honor of Shirley King of Ohio. $12.00 – 15.00.

(c) 6" Spaulding Lloyd Decal Vase. Gold stamp on bottom. Hard to find. A small version of the 10" Juarine vase on page 65. Named in honor of Lloyd Sansoucie of Illinois. $25.00 – 30.00.

Row 3: (a) 4" Royal Copley Linley Decal Planter. Gold stamp on bottom. Harder to find. Named in honor of Linley Carson of Ohio. $12.00 – 15.00.

(b) 8" Royal Copley Betty Decal Vase. Gold stamp on bottom. Hard to find. Named in honor of Betty Carson of Ohio. $25.00 – 30.00.

(c) 4" Royal Copley Joyce Decal Planter. Gold stamp on bottom. Hard to find. Named in honor of Joyce Carson of Ohio. $12.00 – 15.00.

Row 1: (a) and (c) 10" Spaulding Marjorie Decal Vases.
Gold stamp on the bottom. Very lovely. Hard to
find. Named in honor of Marjorie Thorup of
Kansas. $80.00 – 90.00.

(b) 10" Spaulding Juarine Decal Vase. Gold
stamp on the bottom. Very lovely. Hard to find.
Named in honor of Juarine Wooldridge of Missouri.
$80.00 – 90.00.

Row 2: (a) and (b) 8¼" Spaulding Barbara Decal Vases.
Gold stamp on the bottom. Very lovely. Hard to
find. Named in honor of Barbara White of Iowa.
$40.00 – 50.00.

(c) 8" Spaulding Rachel Decal Vase. Gold stamp
on the bottom. Very lovely. Hard to find. Named
in honor of Rachel Osborne of Ohio. $40.00 –
50.00.

Row 3: (a) and (b) 10" Spaulding Shirley Decal Vases.
Gold stamp on the bottom. Very lovely. Hard to
find. Item (a) courtesy of Juarine Wooldridge of
Missouri. Named in honor of Shirley Lehew of
West Virginia. The only difference in these vases
is the "butterscotch" effect on item (a). This is
typical of so many Spaulding decal vases. Some
collectors prefer the lighter color and some the
"butterscotch" effect. $80.00 – 90.00.

(c) 10" Spaulding Juarine Decal Vase. Gold
stamp on the bottom. Very lovely. Hard to find.
Named in honor of Juarine Wooldridge of Missouri.
$80.00 – 90.00.

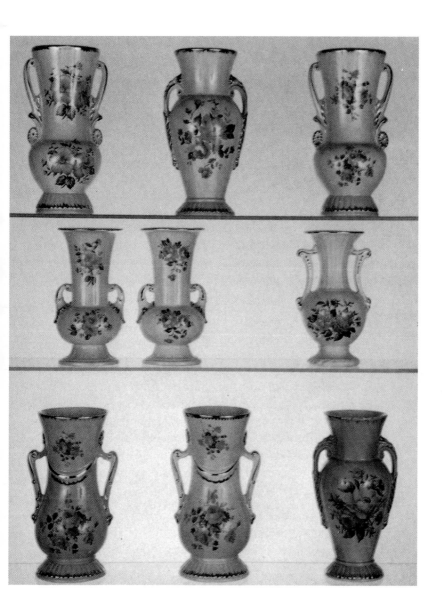

Row 1: (a) 6¼" Royal Copley Blue Beauty Vase. Gold stamp on bottom. Paper label only. Outlined in gold. Not easily found. A pink vase is found in Book I. $12.00 – 14.00.

(b) 7" Royal Copley Virginia Decal Vase. Paper label only. Hard to find. Flat unglazed bottom. $12.00 – 15.00.

(c) 6¼" Royal Copley Floral Handle Vase. Gold stamp on bottom. More easily found. A similar vase in blue is found in Book I. $12.00 – 14.00.

Row 2: (a) 8" Royal Copley Floral Elegance Vase. Green stamp on the bottom. Harder to find. A similar vase in cobalt blue is found in Book I. $20.00 – 25.00.

(b), (c), and (d) 7" Royal Copley Carol's Corsage Vases. Green stamp on the bottom. Other colors can be found in Book I. Not easily found. (b) and (c) $18.00 – 20.00; (d) Cobalt $25.00 – 30.00.

Row 3: (a) 8" Royal Copley Floral Beauty Pitcher. Green stamp on the bottom. Hard to find. Other colors can be found in Book I. $45.00 – 50.00.

(b) 8" Royal Copley Floral Elegance Vase. Raised letters on the bottom rather than a green stamp. Harder to find. $20.00 – 25.00.

(c) 8" Royal Copley Pome Fruit Pitcher. Green stamp on bottom. Very hard to find in cobalt blue. Other colors can be found in Book I. Cobalt $90.00 – 100.00.

We are showing several different coasters on the next two pages and possibly there are many more that haven't surfaced. The coasters consist of ceramic inserts about 3" in diameter with chrome or chrome-like metal rims. The total diameter of each coaster is 4⅝". All coasters were made by Gem in Sebring for Spaulding. There is an additional surprise! Some coasters were made with Sterling silver rims.

It appears that all Royal Windsor coasters were marked whereas the Royal Copley ones had only paper labels.

Row 1: (a), (b), (c), and (d) Royal Windsor Coasters signed on the front or obverse with the following: *Gainsborough by Jon Peter-Amsterdam, Holland.* $35 – 40.00 each.

Row 2: (a), (b), (c), and (d) unmarked Royal Copley Coasters. Show famous Dutch paintings with a woman and a man in a garden setting. One thing to remember, all coasters produced by or for Spaulding did not have a flat bottom, all will have a raised "bump" in the middle. $35.00 – 40.00 each.

Row 3: Unmarked Royal Copley Coasters showing famous Dutch paintings. The name of the paintings, painter, and Amsterdam, Holland, appear on the rim of the insert, which is hard to see. $35.00 – 40.00 each.

69

Row 1: (a), (b), (c), and (d) are Royal Copley Coasters depicting antique automobiles. They are usually unmarked but may be found with a Royal Copley label. $35.00 – 40.00 each.

Row 2: (a) and (b) Royal Copley Coasters like those above in row 1. These depict two more antique automobiles. They were made in sets of four so there are two other makes of automobiles to be found or possibly just different colors of automobiles shown. $35.00 – 40.00.

(c) Unmarked Royal Copley Coasters showing a hunting dog. Also can be found (not shown), are coasters showing pheasants flying and ducks by a marsh. I have not seen the fourth one in this series. $35.00 – 40.00.

(d) Royal Windsor Coaster. On the reverse is found *Exclusively for Frank M. Whiting & Company – FLORAL BOUQUET – Original by Royal Windsor*. Engraved on the rim is *Frank M. Whiting & Co. Sterling*. Usually the Sterling coasters are more expensive. $45.00 – 50.00.

Row1: (a), (b), and (c) Royal Copley Ashtrays. Ashtrays have proved to be very popular items. Most were later items. So few are found. Paper label only. The approximate sizes are as follows: (a) 4½" x 5¾", (b) 5½" x 8", and (c) 5½" x 4¼". (a) and (c) $14.00 – 16.00; (b) 20.00 – 25.00.

Row 2: (a) 6" x 9" Royal Copley Ashtray. Paper label only. Hard to find. Very colorful. $20.00 – 25.00.

(b) 5½" x 8½" Royal Windsor Ashtray. Paper label only. Hard to find. Very colorful. $20.00 – 25.00.

Row 3: (a) 5" x 9" Royal Copley "Butterfly" Ashtray. Paper label only. *U.S.A.* on bottom. Can be found in several colors. $20.00 – 25.00.

(b) 7¾" x 7½" Royal Copley Ashtray. Paper label only. Very colorful. Marked *U.S.A.* on bottom. $20.00 – 25.00.

(c) 6" x 8¾" Royal Copley Ashtray. Paper label only. Most are marked with an incised *U.S.A.* on the bottom. This one has a different "track" design. $20.00 – 25.00.

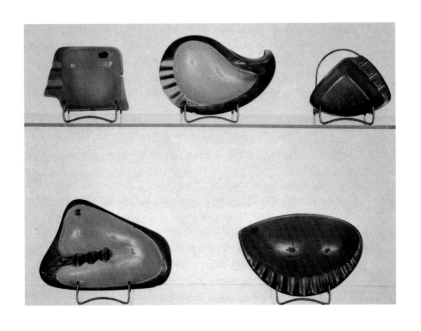

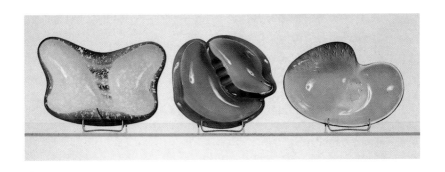

73

Row 1: (a), (b), and (c) Royal Copley Leaf Candy Dishes. They can be found in a wide variety of colors from one color to two colors with white blotches as shown. Found in these three shapes, they are marked with an impressed *U.S.A.* on the bottom. $20.00 – 25.00.

Row 2: (a), (b), (c), and (d) Royal Copley Ashtrays. Paper label only. Very colorful and hard to find. The approximate sizes are as follows: (a) 6" x 4", (b) 5¼" x 4¼", (c) 4⅞" x 3⅞", (d) 5¼" x 4½". $16.00 – 18.00.

Row 3: (a) and (b) Spaulding Ashtray. Item (a) with an impressed fish and (b) with an impressed rooster were both designed by A. D. Priolo as they have his signature on the back along with an impressed © and *U.S.A.* $55.00 – 65.00.

Row 4: Spaulding Ashtray. Almost 7" x 7". *U.S.A.* is found on the back which is typical of many items made at Spaulding. We prize this ashtray because it was the personal ashtray of Morris Feinberg. He picked it up from a table in his study and gave it to us as a gift. $35.00 – 40.00.

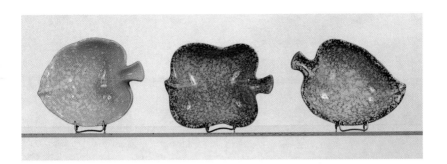

75

Row 1: (a) and (c) are 4¼" Royal Copley Three Tracks
Planters. Paper label only. Two runners. Item (a)
is green whereas item (c) is black. Harder to
find. $16.00 – 18.00.

(b) 10⅛" x 6¼" Spaulding Tray. As you can see
they have a fruit design of an apple and a pear
molded in the bottom of the tray. *U.S.A.* appears
on the back which is typical of many items produced at Spaulding. Hard to find. Courtesy of
Mike Smith of West Virginia. $35.00 – 40.00.

Row 2: (a) and (b) are 10⅛" x 6¼" Spaulding Trays.
Only difference is color shown here in four more
examples. Item (a) is pink and item (b) is green.
$35.00 – 40.00.

Row 3: (a) and (b) 10½" x 6¼" Spaulding Trays. Item (a)
is white and item (b) is aqua. $35.00 – 40.00.

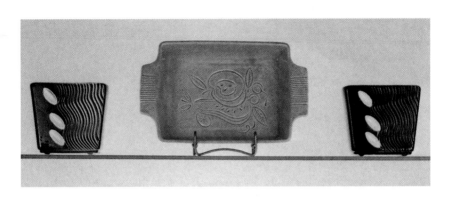

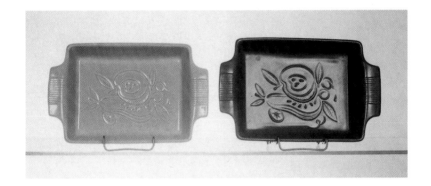

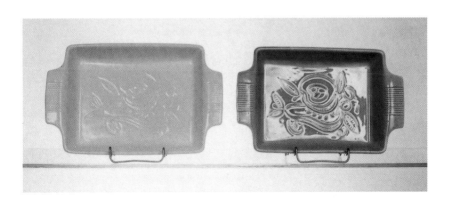

Row 1: (a) 5" x 6¼" Royal Windsor Leaping Salmon Ashtray. Paper label only. *U.S.A.* impressed on the bottom. $35.00 – 40.00.

(b) 5" x 6¼" Royal Windsor Horsehead Ashtray. Paper label only. *U.S.A.* impressed on the bottom. $35.00 – 40.00.

(c) 5" x 6¼" Royal Windsor Rooster Ashtray. Paper label only. *U.S.A.* impressed on the bottom. Unlike items (a) and (b) this item can be found in two color combinations, pink and gray and chartreuse and green. $35.00 – 40.00.

Row 2: (a) and (b) 5½" x 6" "Perching Bird" Ashtray. It looks like the bird has taken a bath and is shaking to dry off. *U.S.A.* impressed on the bottom. Designed by A. D. Priolo. $30.00 – 35.00.

Row 3: (a), (b), and (c) 7½" x 4¾" "Leaping Deer" Ashtray. *U.S.A.* impressed on the bottom, very colorful. Designed by A. D. Priolo. $30.00 – 35.00.

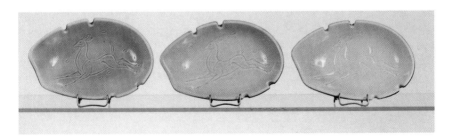

Row 1: (a) 8¾" x 6" Royal Windsor Rooster Hot Pad Holder. Has two holes on the bottom for attaching cup hooks to hang hot pads or pot holders. Designed by A. D. Priolo. Marked with *U.S.A.* on the back. $50.00 – 60.00.

(b) 8¾" x 5½" Royal Windsor Potbellied Stove Hot Pad Holder. Marked *Hot Stuff* on the door of the stove. Like the rooster it has two holes at the bottom. Marked with a raised *U.S.A.* on the back. $50.00 – 60.00.

Row 2: (a) and (b) Stylized Rooster and Hen Planters. Both have two runners and are marked with a raised *U.S.A.* on the bottom. The rooster measures 7½" x 9¼" and has its beak open as if crowing, the hen measures 6½" x 8½" and has her beak closed. White with rose colored specks and lining. $40.00 – 45.00 each.

Row 3: (a) and (b) Stylized Rooster and Hen Planters. Only difference from the ones in row 2, is the color, pink with white specks. Beware of ceramic class copies. $40.00 – 45.00 each.

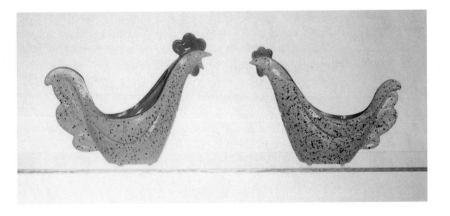

Row 1: (a) and (b) 3" Royal Copley Leaf Handle Sugar and Creamer. Raised letters on bottom but sometimes only a green stamp. Gray with pink handles. This color is hard to find. A yellow pair with brown handles is found in Book I on page 21. $30.00 – 35.00 each.

(c) and (d) 3" Royal Copley Leaf Handle Creamer and Sugar. Raised letters on bottom. Rose and yellow body with green handles. This color is also hard to find. $30.00 – 35.00 each.

Row 2: (a) and (c) 3" Royal Copley Big Blossom Planter. Green stamp. Easy to find. Item (a) has a yellow blossom on a green background whereas item (c) has a pink blossom on a blue background. One with a blue blossom on a pink background is found in Book I on page 19. $10.00 – 12.00 each.

(b) 3½" Royal Copley Floral Arrangement Planter. Green stamp. Easy to find. Another color is found in Book I on page 19. $10.00 – 12.00.

Row 3: (a), (b), and (c) Brass Handled Candy or Tidbit Dishes. Item (a), 7⅞", triangular, has a molded stylized rooster design at each corner with tracks in between. Item (b), 9½", oval, has a molded design featuring stylized fish and sea stars (starfish). Item (c), 7", square, has a molded design showing three different types of leaves. Can be found with tee or ring handles. All have impressed *U.S.A.* ® mark on the bottom. Can be found in a great variety of color combinations from plain one color to two color with or without white specks or "blotches." $25.00 – 30.00 each.

Row 1: Royal Copley Office Samples. Marked with gold stamped lettering under glaze.

(a) and (b) 7¾" Oriental Boy and Girl with Basket on Ground Planters. NPA.

(b) 4¾" Oriental Boy with Big Vase Planter. NPA.

Row 2: China Craft Pebble Glazed items produced with Royal Copley molds after Spaulding closed.

(a) 8" Cocker Spaniel Planter. NPA.

(b) 8" Cat Planter. NPA.

(c) 5½" Teddy Bear Figurine. This is a questionable item. It is thought to have been produced by Stanford Pottery or China Craft. NPA.

Row 3: (a) 8" Cocker Spaniel Planter. Caramel brown glaze. NPA.

(b) 8" Cat Planter. Caramel brown glaze. Both are marked with an incised *U.S.A.* NPA.

(c) 8" Cocker Spaniel Planter. Black and White. All were produced with Royal Copley molds, but it would be pure speculation as to who produced them and when they were produced. NPA.

Office samples were sent between the plant in Sebring, Ohio, and the main office located in the Empire State Building in New York City. They were used to determine what changes if any were to be made. Changes could include design or color. Identical samples were kept at the plant to be used by the personnel there.

85

Row 1: 5" Royal Windsor Plaque Planters.

    (a) Congratulations. $12.00 – 15.00.

    (b) Thinking of You. $12.00 – 15.00.

    (c) Lord's Prayer. $12.00 – 15.00.

Row 2: 4½" Royal Copley Dogwood Plaque Planters.

    (a) The Road to a Friend's House is Never Long (No. 68). $18.00 – 20.00.

    (b) Count Your Blessings — Hold Each One Dear. $18.00 – 20.00.

    (c) Home Is Where the Heart Is (No. 69). $18.00 – 20.00.

    Planters not shown are God Bless This House; Be Happy, Be Gay, For Tomorrow is Another Day; and The Lord's Prayer.

    The dogwood plaque planter was not made for the florist trade. It was designed to introduce the successful Books of Remembrance formula into the chain store outlets.

Row 3: 5" Royal Windsor Plaque Planters.

    (a) Seasons Greetings. $12.00 – 15.00.

    (b) Happy Birthday. $12.00 – 15.00.

    (c) Happy Anniversary. $12.00 – 15.00.

    On an original company brochure two plaque planters are shown: Lord's Prayer No. 211 and Seasons Greetings No. 331.

    All of the 5" plaque planters are part of the Books of Remembrance Series. Another plaque planter To My Valentine can be found on page 53.

Sissy 207 X

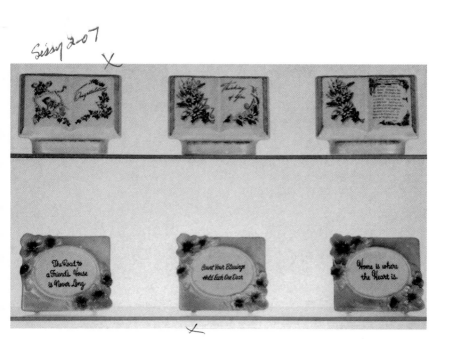

X

Row 1: (a) 5" Royal Windsor Wall Plaque. NPA.

(b) 5" Royal Windsor Planter. $12.00 – 15.00.

The Lord's Prayer. Another style of The Lord's Prayer plaque planter in shown on page 86.

Row 2: (a) The back of item (a) above may have been an experimental item, as the planter has been removed and it has been designed to hang on the wall. NPA.

(b) and (c) 5" Royal Windsor Plaque Planters. Congratulations shown here in pink and blue. $20.00 – 25.00 each.

Row 3: 5" Royal Windsor Plaque Planters.

(a) Mama. This is the only one that has been found to date. NPA.

(b) Happy Birthday. Shown before but not in chartreuse. $12.00 – 15.00.

(c) Happy Anniversary. Shown before but not in chartreuse. $12.00 – 15.00.

All plaque planters are signed *Royal Windsor Books of Remembrance* in gold letters on the bottom.

Row 1: (a) 6½" Deer on Sled. Now known to be produced by Standford Pottery. A similar lamb
planter can be found. NPA.

(b) Resting Deer Planter. It can be found in several colors. Again it is not Royal Copley. NPA.

All items on rows 2 and 3 are copies shown only
to alert you.

Row 2: (a) Kitten Planter. It is a very poor copy of the
Baby Line kitten planter with baby decal made
by Spaulding and shown in Book I. NPA.

Row 3: (a) 7" Swallow. Produced in great quantity and
in many colors. Heavy for its size. Detail is good.
Solid color and solid painted beak. NPA.

(b) 8½" Dog Planter. Very similar to the dog figurine made by Royal Copley. Very heavy. No
planter was made in this dog pattern. Color is
good but inferior to Copley. NPA.

(c) 7¼" Cocker Spaniel Bank. Very light in
weight. Color is atrocious. NPA.

Row 4: (a) and (b) are Mexican Girl and Boy Planters.
Similar in design to Royal Copley's Indian Boy &
Drum Planter. They have three runners and
U.S.A. incised on the back of the planter. Made
by Shawnee Pottery Co. of Zanesville, Ohio. NPA.

These items are shown to help identify non Copley items. As a general rule if it is an animal, a planter, or has runners, then it must be Copley. In book 1 there are clues to help you recognize Royal Copley and non Copley items.

Row 1: (a) and (b) two types of American Bisque Bear Planters. NPA.

Row 2: (a) is an American Bisque Hen with Chicks Planter. A similar rooster planter can be found. NPA.

(b) Seal Planter. This item has long been thought of as Royal Copley because of the similarity of runners. This one has the original manufacturer's label on the bottom between the runners. NPA.

Row 3: (a) shows the characteristic wedge type of runners that identify item (a) above in row 2 as American Bisque. NPA.

(b) is the bottom of the seal planter, above in row 2 (b). Label reads *No. 292 Seal Vogue Art Ware Co. Uhrichsville, OH.* NPA.

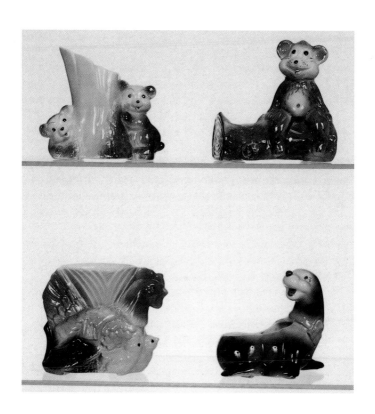

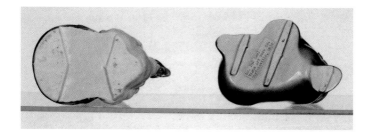

Row 1: (a) and (b) 7⅛" Royal Copley Sitting White Poodle Planter. Paper label only. Hard to find. Item (a) is black whereas item (b) is green. Planter has a diameter of about 5½". $45.00 – 50.00 each.

Row 2: (a) and (b) 6½" Royal Windsor Resting Poodle Planters. About 8½" long. Notice the paper labels. Very hard to find. A blue one has been reported. A lovely addition to the Poodle Series. (a) $60.00 – 65.00; (b) $70.00 – 75.00.

Row 3: (a) and (b) 6½" Royal Windsor Resting Poodle Planters. Item (a) is a dark gray or charcoal, while (b) is a gold trimmed version of item (b) above. (a) $70.00 – 75.00; (b) Priced without gold trim, $70.00 – 75.00.

95

Row 1: (a) 7" Royal Windsor Erect Poodle Planter. Planter is 5½". Paper label only. A pink planter is very hard to find. $70.00 – 75.00.

(b) 6" Royal Windsor Prancing White Poodle on Pink Planter. Not many of this example have been found. $70.00 – 75.00.

Row 2: (a) 7" Royal Windsor Erect White Poodle on Green Planter. Paper label only. Most often found with a Royal Windsor label. All poodle items are hard to find. Three runners. $50.00 – 55.00.

(b) 6" Royal Windsor Prancing White Poodle on Green Planter. Paper label only. This planter may be found with a Royal Copley label. Hard to find. Three runners. $50.00 – 55.00.

Row 3: (a) 7" Royal Windsor Erect White Poodle on Black Planter. Paper label only. This planter may be found with a Royal Copley label. Hard to find. Three runners. $50.00 – 55.00.

(b) 6" Royal Windsor Prancing White Poodle on Black Planter. Paper label only. This planter may be found with a Royal Copley label. Hard to find. Three runners. $50.00 – 55.00.

gift from Sissy X

gift from Sissy X

97

Row 1: (a) and (b) 6¼" Royal Copley Spaniel Figurines. Paper label only. Hard to find. Item (a) is a chocolate brown and harder to find. $30.00 – 35.00; (b) $20.00 – 25.00.

(c) 6½" Royal Copley Airedale Figurine. Paper label only. Hard to find. Listed as No. 4 on an early company brochure. $25.00 – 30.00.

Row 2: (a) 8" Royal Copley Cocker Spaniel Figurine. Paper label only. Harder to find than the planter shown in Book I. $30.00 – 35.00.

(b) 7¾" Royal Copley Dog in Picnic Basket Planter. Paper label only. Very hard to find. Another example of Spaulding's clever retooling. Here the picnic basket has been retooled to include a dog. Like the kitten and bear picnic basket planter, this may be found in pink or blue. $70.00 – 75.00.

(c) 8½" Royal Copley Dog figurine. Paper label only. Hard to find. $35.00 – 40.00.

Row 3: (a) and (b) 8½" Royal Copley Black & White Dog at Mail Box Planter. Paper label only. Very hard to find. A prized item. Notice the only difference is that in item (a) both ears are black. Both are hard to find but with item (a) only a few have been reported. (a) $110.00 – 125.00; (b) $100.00 – 110.00. Item (a) courtesy of Evalee Younts of Iowa.

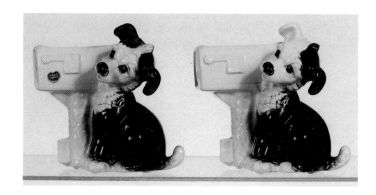

99

Row 1: (a) and (b) Spaulding Lamb on Rocker Planter. Item (a) is red with gold trim and has its hand-painted eyes open while item (b) is blue with gold trim and has its eyes closed. Paper label only like shown on item (b). NPA. Named in honor of Connor Garside of Iowa.

Row 2: (a) 6" Spaulding Deer on Sled Planter (Little Huck). There is a gold trimmed example with fawn spots in Book I, page 83. Notice the Spaulding label. This one was named in honor of Dan Huck of Missouri. $60.00 – 65.00.

(b) 6½" Royal Copley Stuffed Animal Elephant Planter. Paper label only. Two runners. The third member of the Stuffed Animal Series. Very hard to find. $60.00 – 65.00.

Row 3: (a) and (b) Spaulding Pony on Rocker Planter. Item (a) is gray with gold trim and (b) is decorated like the Little Huck deer planter with tiny flower bouquets. Notice the same type of Spaulding label as the previous mentioned items. NPA. Item (a) courtesy of Cathy LeGrand of Illinois.

Row 4: (a) 6" Royal Copley Stuffed Animal Duck Planter. Paper label only. Two runners. A member of the Stuffed Animal Series. $45.00 – 50.00.

(b) 5½" Royal Copley Stuffed Animal Dog Planter. Second member of the Stuffed Animal Series. Paper label only. $45.00 – 50.00.

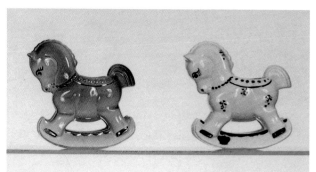

101

Row 1: (a) and (b) 8" Royal Copley Cylindrical Decal Vase. Shown here in pink and blue. *Congratulations* with baby decals. These colors are hard to find. $60.00 – 65.00.

Row 2: (a) and (b) 8" x 6" Royal Copley Decal Vase. No runners. Unusual flared shape. The baby decal with *Congratulations* are always harder to find. $55.00 – 60.00.

Row 3: 8" Royal Copley Cylindrical Decal Vase.

   (a) Lord's Prayer (No. 339), green. $40.00 – 45.00.

   (b) Thinking of You (No. 337), black. $40.00 – 45.00.

   (c) Happy Birthday (No. 336), green. $40.00 – 45.00.

   The 8" cylindrical fish vase shown in Book I on page 57 was retooled to make these vases found in green, black, pink, and blue.

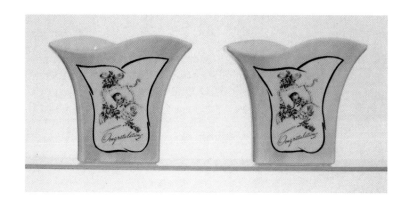

Row 1: (a) and (b) 4⅛" Royal Windsor Baby Mug with Fish Handle Planter. Another member of the Baby Line, they are very hard to find. Notice the Royal Windsor labels. Item (b) courtesy of Bob Harling of Minnesota. $80.00 – 90.00.

Row 2: (a) and (b) 6½" Royal Windsor Erect Poodle Planter. Paper label only. This item is another member of the Baby Line planters. It was listed as No. 364 on a company brochure. Very hard to find. Named in honor of Caleb Holder of Iowa. $75.00 – 80.00.

Row 3: (a) and (b) 7½" Royal Windsor Bunny Planter. These represent No. 366 in the Baby Line planters which consisted of five items. Very rare. Named in honor of McKenna Garside of Iowa. NPA.

Row 1: (a) and (b) 4¼" Royal Windsor Baby Lamb Planters. Paper label only. Very hard to find. This planter was one of the members of Spaulding's Baby Line and listed as No. 363 on a company brochure. The Baby Line consisted of five items. $75.00 – 85.00.

Row 2: (a) 8¼" Royal Copley Small Size Deer and Fawn Planter. Paper label only. Two runners. The regular 9" size is shown in Book I on page 107. Hard to find. $30.00 – 35.00.

(b) and (c) Royal Copley Deer and Fawn With Side Planters. Paper label only. Three runners. Planter (b) is 5⅛" and planter (c) is 3⅛". Item (b) is gold trimmed. Side planters are novel. (b) $35.00 – 45.00; (c) $30.00 – 35.00.

Row 3: (a) 6¼" Royal Copley Palomino Horse Head Vase or Planter. Hard to find in this color. May be found with a green stamp, but usually a paper label. The regular brown colored one is found in Book I on page 81. $35.00 – 40.00

(b) 7½" Royal Copley Deer Open Vase or Planter. Paper label only. Rare in this color. Courtesy of Rocky McReynolds of Florida. NPA.

(c) 6¼" Royal Copley Horse Head Vase or Planter. Very rare in this color. Paper label only. Named in honor of Taylor Devine of Iowa. NPA.

Row 1: (a) 8" Black Cat Planter. Paper label only. My interest with Copley started with this very item. While in college and struggling to find enough money for Christmas gifts, I bought this cat for my father. Only later did I realize it was Royal Copley. I am showing this cat in honor of my late father, Floyd P. Wolfe. $45.00 – 50.00.

(b) 9" Royal Copley Siamese Cats Planter. Paper label only. Found with either a green or brown basketweave planter. The faces were all hand painted, so no two are identical. Very hard to find. $150.00 – 175.00.

Row 2: (a) and (b) 5¾" x 7½" Royal Copley Resting Cat Planters. Paper label only. Item (a) is pure white with pink eyes, making it an albino. It was more than likely decorated this way and sold as a second (refer to page 143), as the tip of left ear has been sanded down making it appear flattened. Item (b) is a light gray with blue eyes, the usual color in which it is found. (a) NPA; (b) $125.00 – 150.00.

Row 3: (a) and (b) 8" Royal Copley Black Cat Figurines. As you can see here, one faces left and the other right. Paper label only. Hard to find. (a) $80.00 – 90.00 each.

(c) and (d) 8" Royal Copley Brown Cat Figurines. The only difference is that of color. They are harder to find than their black counterparts.

Row 1: (a) 7½" Royal Copley Clown Lamp. Paper label only. The planter item (b) was retooled to make this item. Two runners. Very rare. NPA.

(b) 8¼" Clown Planter. The clown items are highly sought after among Copley collectors. Two runners. Paper label only. $75.00 – 85.00.

Row 2: (a) and (b) 6½" Royal Copley Small Angel Planters. There are four differences between these and the two shown in Book I. 1) no hole for hanging, 2) sandals on feet, 3) cord and tassel reaching down the full length of the body, and 4) position of the hands under the chin. Three runners. Paper label only, very rare. $100.00 – 125.00 each.

(c) 6¾" Star and Angel Planter or Candle Holder. Above the hand of the angel is a depression for a candle. Paper label only, three runners. $25.00 – 30.00.

Row 3: (a) 8" Royal Windsor Island Lady Planter. Signed with raised letters on the back. A choice black collectible. Three runners, rare. $100.00 – 125.00.

(b) 8" Royal Windsor Island Man Wall Pocket. The island lady planter was redesigned removing the earrings and the neck and shoulder base. A hole was added for hanging. A rare item, raised letters on the back. $125.00 – 150.00.

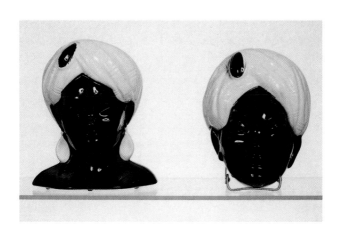

Row 1: (a), (b), and (c) 6¼" Royal Windsor Madonna Side Planters. Raised letters on the bottom. Planter part is about 4". Notice that the hands are crossed in contrast to the other Madonna planters in row 2 and row 3. This planter is very hard to find. $50.00 – 55.00.

Row 2: (a), (b), and (c) 6⅜" Royal Windsor Madonna Planters. Raised letters on the bottom. No other colors have been reported. Listed as No. 349 on a company brochure. Designed, like all other Madonna planters, by Eric Gort. $30.00 – 35.00.

Row. 3: (a), (b), and (c) 8½" Royal Windsor Madonna Planters. Raised letters on the bottom. Size will vary a bit due to mold differences. Listed as No. 351 on a company brochure. $40.00 – 45.00 each.

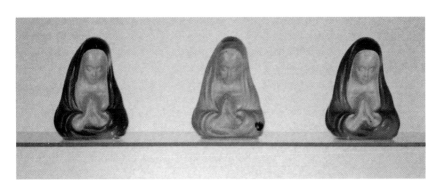

Row 1: (a) 7½" Royal Copley Oriental Boy with Bamboo Side Planter. Unusual. Paper label only. Presence of three runners. Notice that the boy is sitting on a bale of bamboo. Planter is 3½" in height. Hard to find. $60.00 – 65.00.

(b) 7¾" Royal Copley Oriental Girl with Bamboo Side Planter. Mate to item (a). Girl is sitting on opposite side of a taller bale of bamboo. Three runners, paper label. $60.00 – 65.00.

Row 2: (a) 6¼" Royal Copley Boy with Bucket Planter. Rare color — black trousers with blue jacket and hat. The regular colors are found in Book I. Paper label only. Hard to find in this color. $25.00 – 35.00.

(b) 7½" Royal Copley Barefooted Boy Planter. Rare color — tan hat! The regular colors are found in Book I. Paper label only. Hard to find. $40.00 – 45.00.

(c) and (d) 7¾" Royal Copley Child Lamps. Very unusual. This lamp was made by retooling the large angel shown in Book I. Notice that the wings have been removed and a choir hood added. Holes for wiring. Hard to find. Paper label only. $75.00 – 85.00 each.

Row 3: (a) 7½" Royal Copley Chinese Boy with Big Hat Planter Pocket. Rare color — chartreuse hat! The regular colors are found in Book I. Signed with raised letters on the back. Hard to find in this color. $30.00 – 35.00.

(b) and (c) 6¾" Royal Copley Small Chinese Girl and Boy Planters or Pockets. Size is the unusual thing about these planters. Paper label only. Presence of runners. Hard to find. $50.00 – 60.00 each.

114

Row 1: (a) and (b) 6¼" Royal Windsor Teddy Bear with Basket on Back Planter. Paper label only. May be found with a Copley label. $75.00 – 85.00.

(c) 5½" Royal Copley Teddy Bear Figurine. Paper label only. Blue sucker is held horizontally rather than vertically. Some collectors do not think this was produced by Spaulding. NPA.

Row 2: (a) 8" Royal Copley Black & White Teddy Bear Bank. Paper label only. Pink sucker is held vertically. Very hard to find. $150.00 – 175.00.

(b) 6¼" Royal Copley Black & White Teddy Bear Planter. Paper label only. Very hard to find. $60.00 – 70.00.

(c) 7½" Royal Copley Black & White Teddy Bear Planter. Paper label only. Hard to find. $80.00 – 90.00.

Row 3: (a) and (b) 8" Royal Copley Playful Norma in Basket Planters. Shown here with both pink and blue scarves. Paper label only. Very hard to find. The kitten in picnic basket planter in Book I was retooled by substituting a bear for the kitten. Courtesy of Norma and Sherman Lilly of Tennessee. $75.00 – 85.00.

There are some collectors who question whether this item, as well as its kitten and dog counterparts shown elsewhere, was done at Spaulding China because of the lack of crazing, the shape of runners, and overall size. I believe all of them to be Spaulding produced items.

117

Row 1: (a) and (b) 6" Royal Copley Fish Vases or Planters. Item (a) decorated in brown or gray with a red top fin and tail and blue stripe is harder to find than item (b) which is yellow and black with brown stripe. It may be found with or without a decorated eye. Paper label only. (a) NPA; (b) $50.00 – 60.00.

Row 2: (a) Jumping Salmon Planter. As with the more colorful one shown in Book I and the gray one below in row 3, this blue example is questionable. Some collectors don't include them in their collections while others do, just because they were shown in the original books. (a) NPA.

(b) 5" Half-Circle Fish Vase or Planter. Previously shown in Book I but without the attached booklet (closeup shown below) describing the Royal Windsor product line. $45.00 – 50.00 (with booklet).

Row 3: (a) 3¾" Royal Copley Oval Fish Planter. Paper label only. Hard to find. A 5" and a 7" vase in this pattern are shown in Book I. $25.00 – 30.00.

(b) 6½" x 11½" Gray Jumping Salmon Planter. A brightly colored example is shown in Book I. This is a questionable item. NPA.

(c) 5½" Royal Copley Oriental Style Footed. Fish Vase or Planter. Paper label only. Hard to find with a chartreuse background. Another color is shown in Book I. $16.00 – 18.00.

X

grey blue
& tint
Fish

Row 1: (a) 4½" Royal Copley Small Harmony Planter. Paper label only. The Harmony pattern consists of four items: a small planter, a large planter, a vase, and a window box. This shape is found in Book I, on pages 91 & 97 but not in this color. $10.00 – 12.00.

(b) 6½" Royal Copley Large Harmony Planter. This shape is found in Book I, but not in this color. Paper label only. $12.00 – 15.00.

(c) 4½" Royal Copley Harmony Window Box. The only shape of the Harmony pattern not found in Book I. This item is the hardest to find in the Harmony pattern. Paper label only. $12.00 – 15.00.

Row 2: (a) 4¼" Royal Copley Harmony Window Box. Paper label only. Hard to find. The Harmony pattern has become a favorite among collectors. $12.00 – 15.00.

(b) 6½" Royal Copley Black Floral Leaf and Stem Vase. This pattern consists of four items: two vases, a planter, and a window box. Paper label only. The large vase and planter are shown in Book I. This vase is harder to find than the large one. $12.00 – 15.00.

(c) 3½" Royal Copley Black Floral Leaf and Stem Window Box. Paper label only. $14.00 – 16.00.

Row 3: (a) and (c) 4½" Royal Copley Double Spray Planters. This pattern is shown in Book I. Paper label only. $12.00 – 15.00.

(b) 8½" Royal Copley Stylized Leaf Vase. Paper label only. The 5½" vase is found in Book I. $12.00 – 15.00.

Row 1: (a) 5½" Royal Copley Affectionate Birds Ashtray. Raised letters on the bottom. Hard to find. Can also be found in rose and blue and blue on dark blue. $50.00 – 60.00.

(b) 4" Royal Copley Small Bowl With Perched Bird. Green stamp on the bottom. Easy to find. A pink and yellow one is shown in Book I. $12.00 – 14.00.

(c) 5" Royal Copley Lily Pad With Bird Ashtray. Green stamp on the bottom. Easier to find. Can be found in a variety of colors. $12.00 – 14.00.

Row 2: (a) and (d) 5" Royal Copley Leafy Ashtrays. Green stamp on the bottom. Other colors are shown in Book I. Easy to find. $10.00 – 15.00 each.

(b) and (c) 5¾" Royal Copley Bow and Ribbon Ashtrays. Raised letters on the bottom. Hard to find. Item (b) reads *"Put it here, Pal!"* whereas item (c) reads *"Watch those ashes — Friend."* $40.00 – 45.00 each.

Row 3: (a) and (c) 5¾" Royal Copley Bow and Ribbon Ashtrays. Raised letters on the bottom. Another blue one with a different saying is shown in Book I. Hard to find. Item (a) reads *"Lights out, Chum"* whereas item (c) reads *"Old Friends wear well."* $40.00 – 45.00 each.

(b) 5" Royal Copley Straw Hat With Bow Ashtray. Raised letters on the bottom. Hard to find. $30.00 – 35.00.

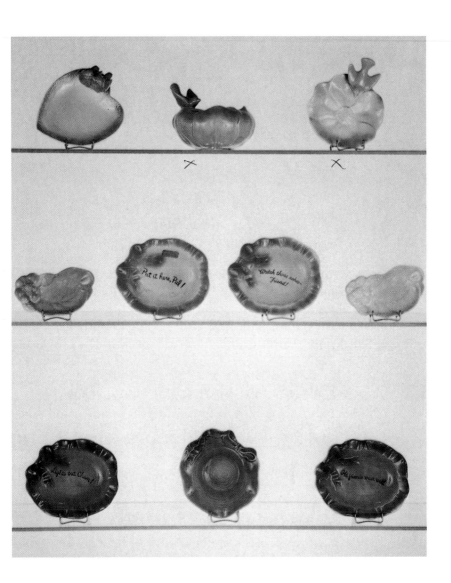

123

Row 1: (a) and (b) 4" Royal Copley Spooks Planters. Paper label only. Item (a) is black and item (b) is green. Harder to find. $15.00 – 20.00.

Row 2: (a) 7" Royal Copley Large, Round Riddle Planter. Paper label only. Harder to find. $25.00 – 30.00.

(b) 4" Royal Copley Oval Riddle Planter. Paper label only. Harder to find. $20.00 – 25.00.

(c) 5" Royal Copley Small, Round Riddle Planter. Paper label only. $20.00 – 25.00.

Row 3: (a) 5" Royal Copley Small, Round Riddle Planter. Paper label only. Harder to find. $20.00 – 25.00.

(b) 4" Royal Copley Oval Riddle Planter. Paper label only. Harder to find. $20.00 – 25.00.

(c) 7" Royal Copley Large, Round Riddle Planter. Paper label only. Harder to find. The Riddle pattern is a favorite among collectors and especially in the black and white. $25.00 – 30.00.

Row 1: (a) 5½" Royal Copley Stylized Leaf Vase. An 8¼" vase is found in Book I. Paper label only. Easy to find. $12.00 – 15.00.

(b) 7½" Royal Copley Marine or Fall Arrangement Vase. Paper label only. Easy to find. Chartreuse background with the plants highlighted in brown. $16.00 – 18.00.

(c) 5¾" Royal Copley Marine or Fall Arrangement Planter. This vase is shown in the black & white section of Book I and listed as No. 20 in the Essex Assortment. Footed and rectangular in shape. Paper label only. $12.00 – 15.00.

Row 2: (a) and (c) Round 4" Royal Copley Wilder Leaf Planters. Item (a) has a black background whereas item (c) has a green background. Pattern shows a triple leaf with a 1½" ribbed margin. Presence of two runners. Paper label only. Harder to find. Named in honor of Alice Karnes of Illinois. $18.00 – 20.00.

(b) 4" x 7½" Royal Copley Trailing Leaf and Vine Planter. Very colorful due to the presence of three colors. Harder to find. Paper label only. Oval in shape with three runners. An 8½" and a 5" vase are found in Book I. $20.00 – 25.00.

Row 3: (a) and (c) Round 5" Royal Copley Laura's Twig Planters. Item (a) has a black background whereas item (c) has a green background. Pattern shows a twig consisting of three leaves. Rather hard to find. Paper label only. Named in honor of Laura Erickson of Iowa. $20.00 – 25.00.

(b) 5¼" Royal Copley Comma Vase or Planter. Presence of three runners. Shape is definitely that of a comma. Very unusual color. Notice the departure from basic colors to that of a runny type of glaze. A later item. Paper label only. Harder to find. $18.00 – 20.00.

+ with gold

All of the planters shown on this page were designed and made for the florist trade. Although of late design they are difficult to find.

Row 1: (a) 4½" Royal Copley Bird Tracks Planter. Paper label only. Gray with pink lining. $10.00 – 12.00.

(b) 3½" Royal Copley Strange Tracks Planter. Paper label only. Boat shaped. Gray with pink lining. $10.00 – 12.00.

(c) 3¼" Royal Copley Bird Tracks Planter. Paper label only. Boat shaped. Light blue in color with pink lining. $10.00 – 12.00.

Row 2: Varying sizes of Royal Windsor planters. All are signed with raised letters on the bottom. Color varies from a charcoal to a gray. Pink lining. Other colors with other linings may be found.

(a) 4¼" Planter and (b) 4¼" Planter represent the small and medium sized planters in this color. $8.00 – 10.00.

(c) 4⅝" Large Planter. Gray exterior. $8.00 – 10.00.

Row 3: Varying sizes of Royal Windsor planters. All are signed with raised letters on the bottom.

(a) 4½" Planter and (b) 4¼" Planter represent the large and small sized planters in this color. Both have a pink lining with a white flocked or stucco effect on the outside. A medium-sized planter of the same color is not shown. $8.00 – 10.00.

(c) 4½" Planter. Other sizes have been seen. This planter is the medium-sized one. Very colorful. This planter has a turquoise lining with a mosaic exterior of white blotches against a turquoise and brown background. $8.00 – 10.00.

Row 1: (a) 4¼" Royal Copley Ivy Footed Planter. This planter has eight leaves rather than seven. Paper label only. Harder to find with eight leaves. Other Ivy planters and vases are shown in Book I on page 21. $20.00 – 22.00.

(b) 6" Spaulding Osborne Decal Vase. Ornate handles. Very hard to find. Gold lettering on the bottom. Named in honor of Lawrence and Rachel Osborne of Ohio. $25.00 – 30.00.

(c) 4" x 7¼" Royal Copley Footed Philodendron Planter. Paper label only. A 7½" footed vase and a small 4¼" footed planter are shown in Book I on page 91. In fact all three items are pictured in the Butler Bros. July 1953 catalog. $12.00 – 15.00.

Row 2: (a), (b), and (c) 3¼" Royal Copley Coach Planter. Some colors are harder to find than others. Two more colors are shown in Book I on page 19. Green stamp on bottom or paper label. $18.00 – 20.00 each.

Row 3: (a) 5½" Big Apple Planter or Wall Pocket. Signed with raised letters on the back and found with paper label. $35.00 – 40.00.

(b) and (c) pair of 3¼" Strange Tracks Candle Holders. They go with the 3½" Strange Tracks planter shown on page 129, row 1 (b). Found with a Royal Windsor label. $20.00 – 25.00 pair.

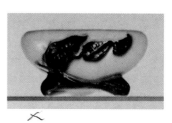

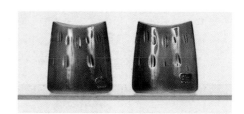

131

Row 1: (a) and (b) 3¼" Royal Copley Plain Jane Planters. Raised letters on the bottom. Found in three sizes and a variety of colors. One of the earlier items which accounts for so few showing up. $10.00 – 12.00 each.

Row 2: (a) and (b) are 5" Royal Windsor Planters or Vases. Similar to the smaller Royal Copley planters above on row 1, but as you can see they have sponge applied gold trim. Paper label only. $25.00 – 35.00 each.

Row 3: (a), (b), and (c) 3½" Royal Copley Rib and Cornice Planters. Notice the three sizes: medium, large, and small. Paper label only. Harder to find. Shown in a July 1953 Butler Bros. catalog. $35.00 – 40.00 set.

Row 4: (a) and (e) 3½" Royal Copley Little Ribbed Planters. Raised letters on the bottom. Green and yellow examples are shown in Book I. Easier to find. $10.00 – 12.00 each.

(b), (c), and (d) are 4⅛" Royal Copley Medium Ribbed Planters. Raised letters on the bottom. Harder to find. A larger planter measuring 5⅛", not pictured, can also be found in a variety of colors. $12.00 – 15.00.

Row 1: (a) and (b) Royal Copley Iron Craft Plant Holders. These were designed to hang on a wall. Item (a) is approximately 6" x 6½" with a 7" chain. Item (b) is 8" in diameter. They both were designed to hold a 3½" Littled Ribbed or Plain Jane planter shown in this book. Like the three types shown in Book I, they also have leaves incorporated into their design. $30.00 – 35.00 each.

Row 2: Close-up of original paper name tag attached to item (b) in row 1. Opposite side of tag reads *"rust proof hand finished."*

All of the planters shown can be found in a wide variety of sizes and color combinations.

Row 1: (a) 2½" x 7¼" Royal Copley Rex Planter. Raised letters. Chartreuse and brown. Hard to find. This item was No. 385 on a company brochure. Named in honor of Rex Sigler of Illinois. $8.00 – 10.00.

(b) 2½" x 6¼" Royal Copley Sectioned Planter. Raised letters. Chartreuse and brown. A rose and brown one is found in Book I. Hard to find. $8.00 – 10.00.

(c) 2½" x 7¼" Royal Copley Hildegard Planter. Raised letters. Rose and ivory. Hard to find. Listed as No. 386 on a company brochure. Named in honor of Hildegard Lary of Illinois. $8.00 – 10.00.

Row 2: (a) 6½" x 7" Royal Copley Footed Vase. Marked with an impressed *U.S.A.* on the bottom found in a variety of colors. Paper label only. $12.00 – 14.00.

(b) 11¾" x 3¾" Royal Copley Planter. A very unusual shaped item. *U.S.A.* impressed on bottom. Paper label only. $18.00 – 20.00.

Row 3: (a) 3½" x 5" Royal Copley Long Tracks Planter. Paper label only. $10.00 – 12.00.

(b) 3½" x 7" Royal Copley Long Tracks Planter. A longer version of item (a). Paper label only. $12.00 – 14.00.

(c) 6⅛" x 5" Royal Copley Bird Tracks Planter. Paper label only. All three items on this row are brown with a chartreuse lining. $12.00 – 14.00.

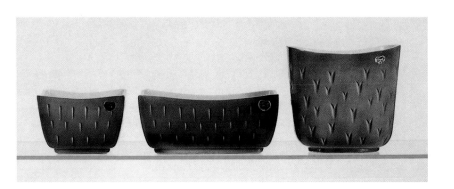

137

Labels

Bibliography and Source Material

Reprints from a 1952 wholesale catalog showing Royal Copley. *Depression Glass Daze*, June 1979. Used with permission of Betty Bell of Verona, Mississippi, and Nora Koch, editor of the *Depression Glass Daze*, Otisville, Michigan.

Personal correspondence with Mrs. James G. Eardley and Charlotte H. Eardley, Berea, Ohio, 1981 and 1982.

Original color charts from the Spaulding China Co., courtesy of Morris Feinberg, Key Biscayne, Florida.

Personal interview with Morris Feinberg, June 7, 1982, at his home in Key Biscayne, Florida.

Personal correspondence and phone conversations with Morris Feinberg, 1981 and 1982.

Phone conversations and personal correspondence with Joe Feinberg, son of Morris Feinberg, September and October 1982.

Personal interview with Margaret Kadisch, Sebring, Ohio, October 1981, and September 1990.

Personal correspondence and phone conversations with Margaret Kadisch, Sebring, Ohio, 1992.

An original brochure showing many items made by the Spaulding China Company, courtesy of Margaret Kadisch.

Lois Lehner, "American Dinnerware and Commercial Pottery," *Depression Glass Daze*, September 1979.

Rena London, Richardson, Texas. Copies of Patents on Pig and Duck Figurines designed by Irving Miller in 1945.

Rena London, Richardson, Texas. Photo of Royal Copley, clips, and personal correspondence, October 1982.

Betty Newbound, Union Lake, Michigan. Article on Royal Copley, *Depression Glass Daze*, August 1982.

Personal correspondence and phone conversations with Anthony Priolo, Santa Barbara, California, 1982, 1990.

Sebring, Ohio: A Brief History of Sebring's 50th Anniversary, Library, Sebring, Ohio. 1949.

Phone conversations with Harry Runyon, former Spaulding China employee, Sebring, Ohio, 1994.

Scenes of Spaulding

Irvin Miller (1898 – 1973) was married to Emma Strauss and had two children, Barbara Miller Henley and Jonathan S. Miller. After the liquidation of Spaulding, he took an active part at the New School (a university in New York that focuses on adult education). He taught courses and served as chairman of the Institute for Retired Professionals there.

Margaret Kadisch (1904 – 1998) was art director for the Spaulding China Co. from the late 1940s to 1957. She has been referred to as "the lady whose fascination with color touched us all."

Dumping various clays and other components of the "slip" (liquid clay) into giant mixing vats. The slip was then carried by pipes to the casting area where it was poured from hoses to fill up the plaster of Paris molds.

Casing and Blocking department where plaster of Paris molds were produced from masters.

Mr. Leonard, manager of the Casing and Blocking Department.

Pouring plaster of paris into master cases to form plaster of Paris molds used in production.

Taking off half of a plaster of Paris mold from case.

Buck (center), manager of Casting Department, with hundreds of production molds.

Scenes of Spaulding

Removing clay birds (ware) just cast from molds. Procedure: plaster of Paris molds are filled to top with slip and after so many minutes (varying with the item being produced), the molds absorb moisture from the slip causing a shell to be formed against the mold walls. When the shell has "dried" to the proper thickness, the mold is dumped (turned upside down), leaving a hollow shell in the mold. The halves of the molds are separated and the ware removed.

Fettling, a procedure in which each clay item has the seam from the mold halves trimmed with a knife and rubbed with a damp sponge to smooth the seam.

Spraying color glaze on sample ducks with Margaret Kadisch, head of the Color and Sample Department, in background.

Tinting wheel where item was put for painting. Each tinter sprayed a different color as wheel brought item in front of her.

Touching up defects in items to be fired a second time and sold as seconds.

Tinted items being dipped in clear glaze (white) with person in foreground wiping glaze from base of item.

Production emerging from circular kiln after being fired.